MY FIRST LEARNING SERIES
SIZE

Written and Illustrated by Caroline and John Astrop

Modern Publishing
A Division of Unisystems, Inc. / New York, New York 10022
Series UPC#: 49525
Printed in the U.S.A.
2 4 6 8 10 9 7 5 3

Mary needs a long hose for the garden.
Is it longer than the worm?
Is the worm short or long?

Which boys have the long pants?

Point to the fattest and thinnest in each row.

Mary's garden is overgrown.
Which plant has the thickest stem
and which has the thinnest stem?

There are two gaps in the fence.
Which is wide and which is narrow?
Can Mary fit through the narrow gap?

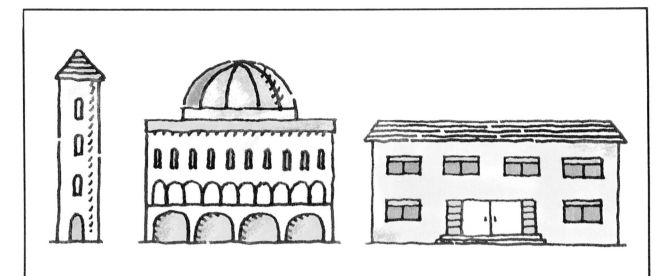

Which buildings are narrow and which are wide?

Match the right-sized hat for each clown.

Mary has put on the wrong boots.
What is wrong with them?
Which are the right size?

Mary has frogs in her pond.
Which one has jumped the highest?
Which one has jumped the lowest?

Who has the highest kite?

Which is the largest in each box?

Mary must pick only the big tomatoes.
How many big tomatoes can you see?
How many small ones?

The apple tree is very tall.
Mary is too short to reach the apple.
How can she make herself taller?

Kitten needs help.
Which teddy bear has the tallest ladder?

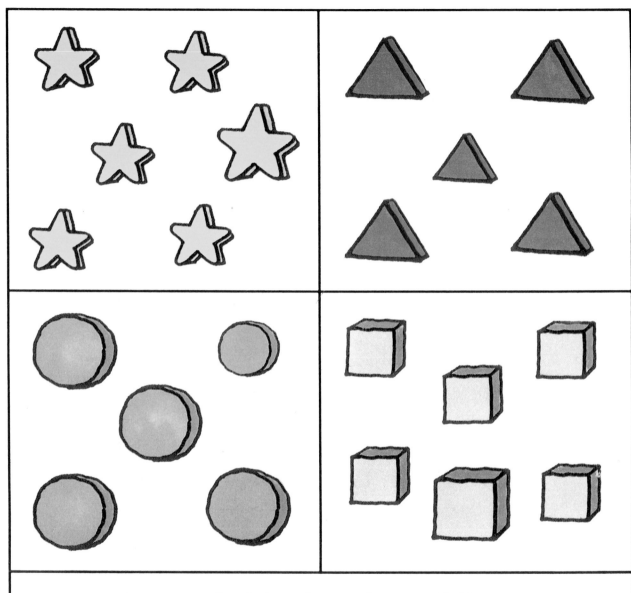

In each square find the shape that's a different size.

Mary's plant is too big for the pot.
Which is the right-sized pot?
What color are the flowers?

Mary is taking care of the tiny seedlings.
What is she doing?
What color is her watering can?

Find a twin for each tiny plant.

Which mouse has the middle-sized tail?

Mary is bigger than the flower.
The flower is bigger than the cat.
Which is the middle-sized one?

Here are some of the words you have learned in this book:

long · garden · short

overgrown · fat · thin

fence · wide · narrow

high · low · pond

big · small · tomatoes

tall · apple · short

kitten · tallest · ladder

big · pot · flowers

tiny · seedling · watering can

bigger · flower · cat

We hope you
enjoyed learning
about
SIZE